THE REAL
Martin Luther

Written by Josh Hamon

Illustrated by Brynn James

First Printing: 2018
ISBN 978-0692960240
Published by The Ministry of War
1281 Sylvan Way #2371
Bremerton, WA 98310
theministryofwar.com
therealmartinluther.com

Ordering Information:
Special discounts are available on quantity purchases by corporations, associations, educators, and others. For details, contact the publisher at the above listed address or email hello@therealmartinluther.com.

U.S. trade bookstores and wholesalers: Please contact hello@therealmartinluther.com

Welcome to Holy Misfits

All of us here at The Ministry of War are pleased as punch to present to you *Holy Misfits: The Real Martin Luther*. The 500th anniversary of the Reformation was on October 31, 2017, making him a timely figure. In many ways, he epitomizes the Holy Misfit.

Before we talk about Martin Luther, let's zoom out. What is a Holy Misfit?

As of this writing, about 2.2 billion people call themselves Christians. You would have a hard time finding something all of them agree on. Those differences can affect how we perceive our heroes of faith. We tend to learn only a small sliver about *our* of the heroes of faith. The good sliver. But, if we hear about *their* heroes of faith, we are sure to learn a healthy dose of what their heroes did or got wrong. The bad sliver.

So, our heroes are _____ and _____. (Holy)
                    positive adjectives
    Their heroes are _____ or _____. (Misfits)
                    negative adjectives

Get it?

The truth is, both sides get it right and both sides get it wrong. So, everyone can learn from each other. That's the heart of this book. Helping you get an introduction to the real person.

Take a moment for yourself — where does Martin Luther fit on the spectrum for you? Is your impression positive or negative?

Our goal here is to provide books about heroes that will humanize them with an honest look at their strengths and weaknesses. We aren't going to be afraid to say that some of the cool stuff you've heard is probably more myth than anything else.

Just as important: Books about *their* heroes will help you to see how these men and women from outside your usual sphere are also worthy of respect, even if they weren't:

neo
post
resistible
paedo
gnostic
millennial
conditional
unlimited

6

limited
half-caff
gluten-free
Christian*

So, enjoy. There is something new to learn about Martin
Luther for everyone in this book. The truth is, there are
awesome and awful things about him that you haven't
learned about. One more thing, just because you are
about to read a history book is no reason that it shouldn't
be enjoyable. If you feel like laughing, laugh.

* Like a good Christian should be.**
** Welcome to my good friend, the footer. This space will be the place for
side comments and other thoughts throughout the book. Not to be confused
with the traditional footnote. This book is anything but traditional.

Oh, wait...

Before I forget. Thank you for buying this book. For quite some time, it has been the constant distraction for the whole team here at The Ministry of War and we hope you enjoy it. We made it just for you; we owe you a high-five.

With sincerity,
Josh Hamon
Word Slinger
The Ministry of War

CHAPTER 1

Let's Divide the Family

Some consider Martin Luther divisive. Apparently, splitting the Catholic Church can give some people that impression. But the truth is, after a significant amount of research,* we can say with complete confidence that:

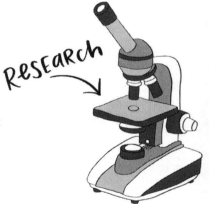

Research

Welcome to the footer; let me give you a quick tour. You are probably used to rather scholarly works in which the footer is used to reference where information came from. This is not that kind of footer. This footer is for thoughts, feelings and asides throughout the book. They are here to make you smile and smirk. Please enjoy responsibly.

* Slipping a museum curator a C-note is my second favorite kind of research.

He was divisive.

By the time the word *Protestant* was first being used to describe Martin's group, he was already dividing his division left and right.

He didn't go looking to divide anything. It was just that he was only agreeable when you agreed with him

Now his friends found him generous, congenial, an excellent host and quite funny. With quick thinking, wit and a large house, he could easily be the life of the party. He didn't tend to shy away from being the center of attention. That is, when he wasn't depressed.

So depressed that the Germans have a special word* for it. He struggled for large parts of his life with depression. It would influence some of his most important relationships and opportunities.

He felt deeply. His joy was great, his sorrow was lamentable and his anger was volcanic.

* The word is *anfechtung*. Good thing Martin was German. Otherwise he might not have had the appropriate word to describe how he felt.

He loved local beer way before it was cool. It helped that he didn't really have access to non-local beer.

While he could be brilliant, he was always stubborn. Once he had studied and decided, that was pretty much it. He argued to prove you wrong. He was not interested in debate as an exchange of ideas.

His enemies found him belligerent, foul-mouthed and onerous. If you accused him of being any of those, he'd blame you for causing him to act that way. So he did agree that at times he was angry with you, but it was, after all, your fault he was angry.

In his writings, he could also be very foul-mouthed.* Which some have defended by saying it was part of the

* Foul-penned?

writing style at the time. This is true, Martin was far from the only person using naughty language. However, Martin took it so far even his friends were sometimes concerned with how potty-mouthed some of his publications were.

The list of people who didn't like him was nearly as long as the list of people he didn't like. What is the German word for cantankerous? The longer this pickle brined, the crankier he seemed to get.

Martin is arguably most famous for going to church on All Hallows' Eve, nailing the 95 Theses to the door and sparking the Reformation. It was actually an attempt at internal reform, not creating a new Christian denomination. You may have heard that, historically, this was the common practice for starting a debate. It was their version of an open letter or a social media post...

... with a nail in it.

Even in English, the poetry shines through:

CHAPTER 1A

Maybe We Should Back Up

Alright, can we back up a hair? Some of you are excited to talk about the big moments, but hold your horses. Some folks need more of the background and everyone needs the whole picture. Actually, Martin Luther was born Martin Luder. He was born a beautiful little cucumber* if ever there was one. The year was 1483 (about 500 years before the author**) and the place was Eisleben, in Central Germany. That's about 175 kilometers*** from Berlin.

* Don't get distracted. Just hold on to this imagery for later.
** Clearly not a coincidence. #destiny
*** Feel free to convert that yourself.

He was one of 8.141592 siblings.* His father, Hans, was trying to get a head start on the 21st century by being an entrepreneur of sorts.

While his family had been farmers, Hans took what money they had and bought a copper mine. Since this was the 15th century, he worked the mine himself and didn't have any investors... so a bit of a passive income fail there. Try not to hold it against him too much; the first stock market wasn't going to get started for almost another 50 years.**

Nothing shows hustle like having a side hustle. So good ol' Pop Hans got a second job managing another mine.

* The decimal is a rather clever way of saying history isn't entirely sure how many siblings he had.
** It would be in Belgium anyway. Although Belgium, as it happens, is a great place to have a copper mine.

18

Working one mine while managing another ended up being profitable enough that he could send Martin to school to get an education. Which was an important step in Hans' master plan to get Martin to become a lawyer.

As the firstborn,* it was the custom that Martin be the one to keep the family's fortunes advancing. However, in Germany, he wouldn't get the family property

That would go to the youngest son. So as firstborn*, he would mostly inherit responsibility and was expected to get a job. Also, someone was going to need to take care of Pops and Ma when they got old.

* Firstborn male. Sorry, ladies, it be like that sometimes.

Maybe We Should Back Up More...

Sorry, didn't back up far enough the first time. Being born in 1483 is actually quite a bit like being born in 1983. It was to be born on the cusp of tremendous change.* You might remember the movable type printing press was invented** in 1450, changing the speed of information by a huge factor.***

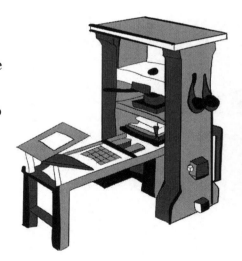

* One could argue that when you're the someone who will change the world, then whenever you're born is the cusp...
** Why doesn't Bi Sheng get the credit when he invented it 400 years earlier?
*** At the height of the Renaissance, it was about 90 times faster.

Other notable inventions around the birth of our li'l cucumber:

The muzzle-loading rifle was invented in 1475, changing the speed* at which we could hurt each other.

The parachute was invented in 1485. Safety first! The first glider test wouldn't be documented for another 406 years (and unfortunately, Otto** was unable to combine his glider with the parachute.)

* And accuracy.
** Otto Lilienthal is the OG (original gangster) when it comes to flying.

The first copyright was granted in 1486 — not that Martin would really cash in on it.*

Here's one you probably know — Columbus sailed the ocean blue in 1492.**

* Didn't he know that he was supposed to make sure the family moved up economically and/or socially?
** Okay, not an invention. Unless three rights makes a left is an invention. As applied to Columbus: he invented the test to the hypothesis "the best way to get east is to go really, really far west."

Going back to the movable type printing press: this lone invention was essential for Martin in two ways.

First, it gave him access to books in general and to specific books that would deeply influence him.*

While he preferred the sermon to the book, he wrote down quite a lot of what he had to say. The printing press made more of what he had to say, more accessible, to more people. We have a large amount of his writing still extant (still physically existing) including thousands of sermons, letters, etc.

Second, he came of age far enough after the invention of the press that literacy rates were starting to improve as access to books improved. After all, the day after the printing press was invented, literacy had not improved. But add half a century and you'll start to see some improvement in not just the speed of information being shared but also in the overall level of education. The books would be available and more people would be able to read them.

He was born between the Middle Ages and the Renaissance. It might not be possible to express how important this was.**

* One of those books was written by Erasmus.***
** Probably can't be over-expressed, so expect some more expressing.
*** If not yet, later you'll find out how shocking this information is!

CHAPTER 1C

Back to the Story You Came For

Did we leave Martin at school? In any case, let's pick it up there. When Martin was around age 5, the family moved to Mansfeld and Martin began attending school. Eventually he headed off to Magdeburg for further school, then to Eisenach.*

* Not to be confused with his hometown of Eisleben.

24

For university, he went to Erfurt, receiving his BA in 1502 (at age 18) and MA in 1505.* Here in Erfurt, he gave his family name a Latin twist. In Eisleben, Martin Luder was born; in Erfurt, Martin Luther was born.

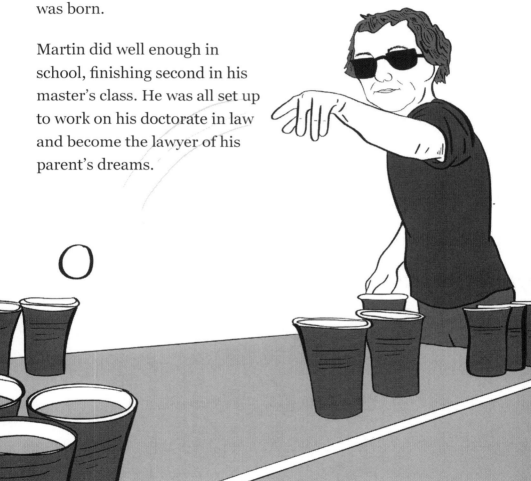

Martin did well enough in school, finishing second in his master's class. He was all set up to work on his doctorate in law and become the lawyer of his parent's dreams.

* You can do this. If he got his first degree three years ago, and three years ago he was three years younger than the legal drinking age in the United States, then how old is he when he got his second degree?

25

it's A TaLe as OLD AS tiME

Parents have children.

They walk 15 miles* in the snow uphill both ways.

They do everything they can to give their kids opportunities they never had.

They want their children to become lawyers.* Pops Hans was no exception.

* Always specifically lawyers, too. Doctors got added later, if you want to get all totes *ad fontes* about it.

Children dutifully got law degrees and became lawyers, thereby making their parent's sacrifices not in vain.

Oh wait, that's not how the story goes.

Children don't understand the parents' point of view and do something different.

* Ah, much better.

Before his pops got into copper mining, the family was in the agricultural trade.*

There is no indication that Martin had a different plan than his parents at this point. But while he killed it academically, he struggled personally. His lawyer training was honing his ability to declare himself guilty before God.

* Not to say they performed the work of farming; they owned land that farms were on.

Remember the German word for deep depression/anxiety/trial/affliction? The dreaded *anfechtung*, although in Martin's case we'll use the plural *anfechtungen*. Many feel English doesn't do the word justice. Martin often struggled with the anxiety of weighing his sins against his graces and losing. Seeing himself as sinful inspired him to fear* God.

That is, until...

* And in this case, a fear that led to hate. Yoda taught us what happens when fear leads to hate.

31

He Got Caught in a Thunderstorm.

It's a tale as old as time:* A man prone to anxiety got into a situation. When suddenly, the situation becomes of a life-threatening nature. So then he had to decide what he would do, or at least how to properly defend himself from lightning bolts when all he had was a horse and some books. He also might be concerned that this wasn't a natural storm, but God's judgment.

* Actually it's another tale as old as time.

Out of fear and desperation, he made a promise to the higher power he thought would be pertinent to the danger. Martin couldn't beat the storm, but he could pray to someone who could mediate on his behalf. He had to find someone and fast because lightning bolts are also very fast.

On July 2, 1505, that's how it goes. Riding back to Erfurt from a trip to visit the family in Mansfeld, Martin got caught in a thunderstorm. Terrified and possibly struggling with anfechtung, Martin might have thought the storm was God's judgment for his sins. He made a deal/plea to Saint Anne:

"Saint Anne save me! My life for the monkery!"*

st. anne

* This is not a quote. Martin didn't speak modern English, "monkery" is just fun to read, even though it's not a real word.

interlude

Who is Saint Anne?

By tradition she is the mother of Mary, and Jesus' nana. Also the patron saint of miners. So, no surprise, she's a saint that this family was keenly interested in.

end interlude

Martin does actually keep his part of the bargain, and after setting his affairs in order he presents himself to the Augustinian Order. His parents see years of hard work put into their firstborn* thrown away over a lightning strike or two.**

* Firstborn male.
** And he didn't even get zapped as far as we know.

CHAPTER 2

Get Thee to a Monkery

However Martin might have felt in the moments between lightning strikes, he showed he was going to make more than good on his vow and became a monk's monk joining the Observant Augustinian Order.* There were certainly other, less hard-core, orders available to him.

Not all monastic lifestyles were equally ascetic. (Asceticism is a difficult-to-pronounce word that means practicing self-denial for spiritual purposes.) He jumped right into the order and their practices. Really fun stuff like:

* The monks are divided into different orders. Some less fun than others.

NO WIFI*

SILENCE

SLEEPING IN THE COLD

FASTING

AUSTERE DIET**

NO REINDEER GAMES

* Well, technically the whole world was taking a fast from wifi since wifi didn't technically exist.

** An austere 16th century monk diet.

39

But joining the order was about more than prayer and penance. In 1507, he was ordained (became a priest) and performed his first Mass. Marking the special occasion, his father showed up, though it was probably to get this son back on the legal path. Martin didn't budge.

Even rigorous monk life was no cure for his difficult-to-translate depression. No records survive of any complaint or discipline against him at a local or regional level.* And while the source isn't unbiased, he did say, "If anyone could have gone to heaven through monkery, it would have been [Martin]."**

* At the international level, let's just say, things ended a teeny bit differently.
** Yep, he said it about himself. #humblebrag

He was so devoted to the disciplines of his order, that he was noticed by the leader of a German branch of the order, the Vicar General (a bishop's chief deputy) of Germany, Johann von Staupitz. (We'll call him General V.) However, General V didn't just notice Martin's lean-in approach to monk life, he also noticed that Martin was spiraling in the wrong direction. The more Martin confessed and did penance, the more he seemed to sink into depression. So he encouraged Martin to further his education.

After all he had performed well there in the past. In 1509, he would receive a second degree, this time in biblical studies in Wittenberg. General V was beginning to see that being a hermit or a priest wasn't going to be the life for Martin.

While Martin's grades were above average, education wasn't working the way General V had hoped. Studying the Bible didn't seem to lift Martin's spirits.

Resolute, General V tried something else. In 1510, he sent him on a pilgrimage to Rome. It was the center of

REPORT CARD

B+

dude NEEDS to CHILL out

Christendom and would also add depth to his biblical studies. A place steeped in history, beauty, glory, a lot of stained glass and the work of the saints. Here he could see beyond his monk's cell or university library.

ST. PAUL

To be honest, while Rome was the bee's knees in Martin's time, during Saint Paul's life time, he had a little bit more of a love/hate relationship with the place. Since, by tradition, it was also the place of Saint Paul's death.

Getting there was half the fun, and after so many years (and so many pilgrims) many monasteries were well positioned along the way. This meant, on the journey to Rome, Martin would have been preparing himself spiritually to visit the beloved city.

It must have been beautiful. Ever since the time of Pope Nicholas V (1447-1455), the city had been upgrading.* In Martin's day, Pope Julius II was no slouch, he was a patron of the arts and had been transforming the city. When Martin went to visit in 1510, Michelangelo** was halfway through painting the Sistine Chapel.

There is no evidence Martin got to see the chapel and likely he wouldn't have been fond of it if he had. Though, it is easy to imagine him taking a peek while Michelangelo was on a break:

* Before that, the city was on a severely deferred maintenance program.
** Not the Ninja Turtle, the Italian. Easily confused because they both loved pizza. Never mind, that doesn't explain anything, everyone loves pizza.

"Martin, what do you think of it so far?" Michelangelo asks.

Martin responds excitedly, "It's really amazing, I'm so impressed. Is it okay if I ask a question?"

Michelangelo smiles, "Of course."

His experience in Rome can be typified with one particular site: Scala Sancta. A definite must-see, especially for first-time pilgrims to Rome. By tradition, they are the marble steps of Pontius Pilate's praetorium. In this particular context, praetorium means palace. Emperor Constantine had them moved to Rome as a gift to his mama Helen. True story.

For the pious, here was a chance to walk where Jesus walked, without going to the Middle East.

So Martin got in line, made an offering* and then walked up the steps on his knees. It was very common for people to pray the rosary while ascending.

* Try not to see this like he bought a ticket to wait in line for a ride at Disneyland. Martin wouldn't have felt that way, partially because there was no Disneyland and partially because with that many people, lines will just form.

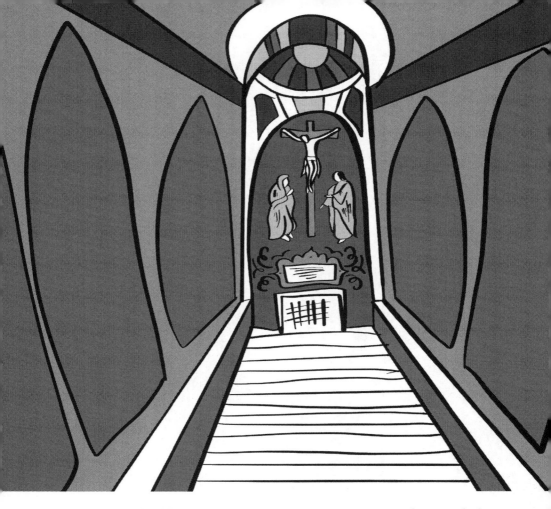

Instead of having a mountaintop experience, he was left with only angst and achy knees.

At best, he found Rome to be a letdown. Later in life, he would call it some very mean names.* It wasn't at all what he was expecting. Life in the austere monastery wasn't a preamble for Rome, it was the antithesis. When he returned, General V learned that his plan hadn't worked out so well.

* Including, but not limited to: ^&$#, &(#!$, !@#$!@#$ and ##$##%!

48

Since the contemplation of cloister life and pilgrimage seemed to deepen Martin's depression, General V sent him back to school, because he seemed less unwell there.

He returned to Wittenberg and received his doctorate in theology in 1512. Martin then took a position as a lecturer at the university. He remained a monk and was charged with preaching to the Black Order* (the Augustinian monks there wore black robes).

* If you've been looking for a band name complete with historical context, you're too late. Black Order is taken. However, they could probably still use a preacher.

For someone given to a kind of depression with no comparable English translation, he apparently took to lecturing like a child to high fructose corn syrup.

The Elector of Wittenberg, Frederick the Wise (Freddie Dubs*) was happily surprised to find himself with a theology professor that was a cure for insomnia. A man of the times** who was funny and thoughtful.

For preaching he started with:

* A rough American translation of Frederick the Wise.
** Which is to say, a professor who wasn't unwilling to poke at things.

Martin unexpectedly began to find some relief from anfechtungen in preaching. He found, as many do, that he was preaching to himself as well as to the Augustinian monks in his charge.

He would never return to quiet, private monkery life. Martin would charge right through preaching the Psalms going next to Romans and then Galatians. The world too, was in motion...

A Moment in Time, an Exhale and an Inhale

While you've already heard a monologue on the importance of the technological changes during this time period, you haven't heard all of the repercussions of time and technology. Let's zoom in on 1513 through 1517.

1513: Pope Julius II dies. He is succeeded by Giovanni di Lorenzo de' Medici (Leo X*). According to some, Julius II is a patron of the arts and not of bookkeeping — leaving Leo with debt. Leo and Julius do agree on the importance of arts and the building up of Rome.

* Which is not pronounced Leo Ex, but Leo the 10th, not as cool.

Which is to say, Leo didn't look at the books, see a lot of red ink and take austere measures to ensure financial reform. Instead, he kept on keeping on.

iNTerlude

Time to talk about indulgences, the "I" word. Non-Catholics, please refrain from getting on your high horses at this time. Catholics, this is not a trap or a tirade.

For many, indulgences aren't what you think they are or were. There will be a quick history of indulgences in a moment, but first most of you need to reset what you think of when you hear the word indulgence.*

Remember that, as with any idea, not everyone agrees on it. Even if they have the same affiliation. Therefore, if you gathered 100 people in a room — who call themselves good Catholics and who believe in indulgences — you would get multiple definitions. Here's one that is useful for our context. The logic of indulgences:

1. People will do bad and not do good.

2. This is quantifiable. (If I punch you in the face. I've sinned once. If I then steal your purse, that's a separate sin. 1 sin + 1 sin = 2 sins)

---

* Unless you're thinking about eating some sort of decadent dark chocolate dessert. Then your definition is probably totally fine. This interlude is about something different.

3. Actions have consequences.* These aforementioned actions put things askew. Between you and me, and between God and myself.

4. Those consequences vary. We are going to leave God out of this for a bit and just talk about you and me, because indulgences are about earthly and temporal consequences.

5. Say I ask you for forgiveness. Say you do forgive because you know how sincerely sorry I am that I punched you. Forgiveness doesn't necessarily mean there are no more consequences for me.

6. Which is a bummer because now I'm being arrested. That's the temporal consequence of punching someone.**

7. To escape the consequences of my actions on earth, I need to receive an indulgence. Some people have sufficient graces (remember Saint Mary is full of grace) as opposed to sins. That's the indulgence. So Saint Mary can grant an indulgence. Part of being a capital 'S' Saint means you have graces available.

8. The church has a treasure trove of grace available to them to grant as indulgences. Also, they have the keys to unlock the chest.

* So Newton will "discover" in 1686.
** The forgiveness is appreciated.

9. An indulgence isn't eternal forgiveness.*

10. An indulgence can only remove temporal or earthly penalties. This had been codified long before Martin was born.

11. Added bonus, you can get indulgences for others, including people already dead.

Show me the money, you say? There used to be money involved, though technically you never "bought" an indulgence. At some point early on, alms-giving (donating to those in need) got connected to the practice. It's easy to imagine it starting off well-intentioned. Remember, you received the indulgence from the bounty of grace available, no dollars required. Eventually, money became part of the standard practice. The check you wrote still said "building fund" as opposed to "indulgence #964056 for being naughty."

There is a school of thought that feels all indulgences started off in the 11th century as an enticement to join the crusades. Joining the crusade granted you an indulgence however, you could receive the same indulgence without joining the crusade... if you could just make a donation...

* Truly, this is only a partial explanation. It's quite a deep subject as to where they come from and how they are measured. But it's time to wrap up this interlude. TL;DR:** Indulgences, as Protestants tend to learn about them today, aren't what they started out as and isn't what they are today. But Protestants still get really upset like nothing has changed in 500 years.
** Too Long; Didn't Read:

Regardless of when or how the money showed up, it was officially abolished in 1567 by Pope Pius V. In some circles, that might even be considered a reform.

Even in the Catholic Catechism of 1471, it was clear that an indulgence didn't cause God to forgive you in a get-out-of-hell way. We'll revisit this later in the chapter. However, there's what the catechism said and there's what the guy offering indulgences said.*

end interlude

So, Leo X says to himself something like, "I've inherited a huge debt and I'd love for Rome to be cooler when I die than when I arrived... time to invent the building fund."**

Now that the interlude is over and we're back on track: The takeaway right now? The Pope changes in 1513. The new Pope takes on more debt and starts a building fund. Which increases some people's temptation to abuse indulgences.

Which we'll get to in a moment.

---

* Also, remember the 16th century still had lots of non-readers. And of the reading group, how many of them could read Latin? Which was probably what the catechism (and the Bible) is written in.
** Leo X didn't say this. Not only because he didn't speak modern English but also because the building fund had already been invented.

You know what else? Remember that pesky printing press? Well, darn it, nothing seems to stop it. Technology is like that sometimes. In 1516, it printed another book. One that will inspire Martin and change the world.

Of all things, it was written by (the already famous and humanist OG) Desiderius Erasmus Roterodamus.*
So D.E.R. had already published half a dozen works by

* Erasmus to history. For the rest of the book we're going to use his rap name the D.E.R. berüchtigt.**
** It's funnier in German, we'll just call him D.E.R. Yes, he's not even German. Nobody's perfect after all.

this time, including his most famous one: *The Praise of Folly* in 1511. In 1516, he publishes something that is arguably more impactful on history.*

He released the *Novum Instrumentum Omne,* (which is now considered to be part of the *Textus Receptus*) a parallel Greek and Latin translation of the New Testament.

* Not sure who's arguing this point, but there's probably some poor uninformed soul out there. They just need a copy of this book to clear things up. Help 'em out would ya?

If the Renaissance had a battle cry, it was: ad fontes!*
"[Back] To the sources!"** For hundreds of years the
Bible was read in any language you'd like, as long as it
was Latin. The number of folks who could now speak
Greek, Hebrew and Aramaic was growing because it was
becoming fashionable to read the works of antiquity in
their original languages. For more than a hundred years,
you would study other people's studies of something, not
the work itself. We *might* do a similar thing today where
we "study" someone's blog post about something instead
studying it for ourselves.

It was 1516, Martin has had a degree in biblical studies for
five years. He's a monk, yet it was like he's never read the
Bible at all. The humanist D.E.R. had put the "New" in
New Testament and everything was about change.

Martin got himself a copy and started reading. It
caused him to question the Vulgate, the reigning Latin
translation. He was shocked*** when he read that
Matthew 4:17b had been translated as "Do penance, for
the kingdom of heaven is at hand." Instead of "Repent,
for the kingdom of heaven is at hand." Martin found this
to be a mistranslation of Jesus' words.

---

* Which wouldn't really make your enemies tremble in fear. So either choose
a different war cry for yourself or try not to have enemies.
** *Back* is implied, it literally means "to the fountains."
*** For someone with four academic degrees, two of which have to do with
the Bible, it's shocking he was shocked.

DO PENANCE
~~repent~~

In this moment the relatively new movement of humanism would make its largest contribution to Protestantism. Did they intend this to happen?

Dear Humanity,
Though our intentions were most pure, we must apologize for our unintentional part in the Reformation. We thought that by exposing the Bible to primary sources we would make the world more Human-centric. We had no idea this would happen
We are ever so sorry.
Regretfully,
Humanism

There were two local events that got Martin's dander up. Yes, they were all about indulgences.

Freddy Dubs had been collecting relics (items belonging to past saints.) He planned to do an exhibition on November 1, 1517 as a celebration of All Saints' Day. He would get a cut of the entrance fee, to help pay for more relics. Part of the proceeds would go to Rome, which they appreciated. He published a catalogue of his collection* that contained more than 17,000 relics, including a crucifixion nail and some of the Virgin Mary's breast milk.

* People who saw the collection would receive a special indulgence that would reduce purgatory time by 1.9 million years.

Johann Tetzel had been recruited by the Archbishop Albert of Madgeburg to dispense indulgences.

When Mr. Tetzel arrived, he was forced to camp across the river, Freddy Dubs didn't want any competition. Still, plenty of the Martin's parish went to check it out.*

* If you were selling indulgences and across the river someone had a special indulgence measuring almost 2 million years, doesn't it seems like bad business to go there at all? How can you compete with that?

While Martin was now a full-grown cucumber, he was still brining. No one would argue that he already had more than enough vinegar in him to be more than a little frustrated. While we've already done a little discourse on what an indulgence is, remember that what the catechism says and what the person preaching indulgences says don't necessarily line up.

From Martin's perspective people were showing up with official pieces of white paper saying they were forgiven of everything ever. People felt like they could buy their way out of hell. The scandal around Tetzel gets way past

PG-13 pretty fast and it was hard to parse out the history from all the vitriol.

What is clear is that Martin felt the issue was less about the money and more about what he perceived as indulgence preachers lying to people about forgiveness. As a response, he sat down and wrote out his thoughts for publication.

Now we get to the legen*dary event.

* Wait for it.

CHAPTER 3

I Got 95 Theses

(LET'S DEBATE EACH ONE)

Some readers know what's coming next. October 31, 1517 is his most (in)famous moment. He nails his 95 Theses to the church door. How did it go down? Was it a dark and stormy night that October? Did he get interrupted by trick-or-treaters? What brand of hammer did he use?

Protestant View

Catholic View

Agnostic View

(Did this really happen?)

There are reasons to doubt the specific act of attaching paper to a door via a nail. At the very least, it shouldn't be taken as gospel.

Two main reasons:

1. The first recorded mention of the event is after Martin's death by Philip Melanchthon, who didn't witness the event. They were bests buds, whether that counts for him or against him as a source is up to you.

2. Martin was a man of the cloth, in the *business* and didn't need to use the "make a suggestion box." He knew where to send things if he wanted to discuss it. We do know that he did have copies sent to Archbishop Albert. (Who then forwarded them to Leo X.)

But before you throw out tradition right along with the baby's bathwater:

1. He did hold a doctorate and starting debates this way was one of the perks.

2. In the heading of the 95 Theses, he invited scholars from other cities to weigh in. If it was meant to be an internal document, then it probably would have been addressed to the Pope or other specific persons for review, not all scholars anywhere.

One more thought that isn't necessarily for or against the historical accuracy of Martin nailing the 95 Theses to the door is that he had already written publicly against indulgences. So the 95 Theses wasn't his first rodeo. Just the first time he nailed it to the door, or the first time he sent an internal memo.

More important than how the 95 Theses reached the masses is that they did. Martin certainly didn't have any idea of the repercussions to follow.* So it's unnecessary to add magic to the moment as if he knew the future. He posted the 95 Theses in between going to the supermarket and picking up his dry cleaning, not with WWE-style theatrics.

Due to a severe lack of fax machines during this era, it would be a while before the Pope wrote an official response. In the meantime, General V sent Martin to the Heidelberg to further discuss his ideas.

So Martin drafts another 28 (well 40**) theses and takes them in May of 1518 for a meeting of the Augustinian Order.

* He had already written other pieces in 1517 about the abuse of indulgences and hadn't become an infamous international outlaw. What's a few more theses?
** He brought 40 theses with him but 12 are about Aristotle, so history remembers them as the 28 Theses.

28 MORE... here we go

Here Martin gets away from specifically critiquing indulgences and papal authority to deep dive into issues that would become the heart of the Reformation. Reading the 28 Theses will sound very modern to the reader, especially if they are from a Lutheran or Reformed background.

Technically, this is known as the Heidelberg Disputation, although only he was disputing. In the modern vernacular, we might think of it as closer to The Heidelberg TED Talk™. In attendance is John Calvin's future mentor Martin Bucer.

THE ·H·E·I·D·E·L·B·E·R·G· TED Talk

Wanting to put the dispute back in disputation, Cardinal Thomas Cajetan brought Martin to Augsburg in October of 1518. Cardinal Tom did what any self-respecting cardinal would do in the face of a mere monk trying to say the world is upside down and it's the Catholic Church's fault. It only took one word:

This is the first real opposition Martin faced. Had our full-grown cucumber finished brining? How would Martin handle his first do-or-die challenge?

Yeah, so he runs away. Back to Freddie Dubs. (At Wittenberg he's free to continue preaching and writing.)

Another disputation followed in July of 1519 in Leipzig. This time Johann von der Ecken* went to debate Martin's teachings. Disputations do work a little better when people talk back and forth during the same disputation.**

Now Ecken has an interesting tactic:
He debates Martin's Theses. But he debates them with Andreas Bodenstein von Karlstadt who is Martin's mentor at the university.

---

* He's probably not the inspiration for the Pokemon™ Ekans.
** Otherwise would it be *Sola Disputation?*

JOHANN VAN DER ECKEN VS ANDREAS BODENSTEIN VON KARLSTADT

After a couple of weeks, it was clear that Mr. Andreas couldn't hold his own.* Mr. Ecken didn't just have the backing of the Pope, he was also a skilled debater. Martin decided he needed to get in the ring on his own behalf.** A rather bold move considering last time he ran away when faced with serious opposition.

---

* Take a moment and imagine how utterly grateful/sad you are that Presidential debates don't go on for weeks. The reality is, if you want to watch lengthy debates, it's something called CSPAN. Use your fax machine to learn more.
** Like a boss.

JOHANN VAN DER ECKEN VS MARTIN LUTHER

When you craft 100+ theses and quite a few have to do with challenging papal authority, you can expect the papal authority to want to talk about it. Mr. Ecken already proved himself ready for this theology slam. How the debate actually ended requires some interpretation.

Let's do a quick examination from a couple of perspectives. For bonus points, grab a friend and read aloud.* For the sake of time, we'll skip to the end:

* Whoever has a better gravelly superhero voice gets to read for Martin because the book is about him.

Catholic reenactment first.

* Jan Hus was executed by the Catholic Church for his beliefs.
Ecken's statement is not trying to be subtle.

Now for the Protestant reenactment.

* Athanasius (296-373) was an early church leader that everyone agreed was big deal.

In both versions of Leipzig you can hear for the first time what will become *Sola Scriptura*. The first of what will be five* solas. *Sola Scriptura* (scripture alone), *Sola Gratia* (grace alone), *Sola Fide* (faith alone), *Solus Christus* (Christ alone) and *Soli Deo Gloria* (glory to God alone.)

Martin had left the disputation at Augsburg a non-Christian and arrived at Leipzig to dispute with Ecken converted. When did Martin become a Christian? Take a moment and let it sink in: he nailed the 95 Theses while a non-Christian, before he went on to write 28 more, still as a non-Christian.**

* Try not to hold it against Martin that he missed the 6th sola. *Sola Wifi*, 5 out of 6 is pretty good.
** This will be a big shock to many readers, like discovering Saint Patrick isn't Irish. (Except on Saint Patrick's Day, when everyone is temporarily made Irish.)

Saint Patrick

Later in life, Martin writes about when he was converted. Specifically, he sees his own heart change about what the righteousness of God means. Martin went from hating the righteousness of God, to loving it.

Martin was preaching through the Psalms a second time early in 1519, while personally studying through the Book of Romans. Specifically, Romans 1:17:

the righteous will live by faith

ROMANS 1:17

For him, this was rediscovering another sola. *Sola Fide*, faith alone. Salvation was no longer a heaven or hell math equation. Martin's only mediator was God, earthly consequences be damned.

Ladies and gentlemen, our little cucumber has become the pickle he was meant* to be.

* Some people would prefer "he chose to be" or "God foreknew him to be." But Martin didn't believe in free will.

CHAPTER 4

I Can Write Chapter Books

After Leipzig, Martin's time as monk was drawing to an end. It's almost surprising how long it took. After all, you can't be in the club if you keep breaking the first rule.*

* The first rule of monk club: don't talk about what's wrong with monk club.

A year after his argument with Ecken, the public decree, or papal bull,* was issued. (The seal used to authenticate the document was called a bulla.) Officially titled *Bulla contra errores Martini Lutheri et sequacium* (Bull against the errors of Martin Luther and his followers), history knows it as *Exsurge Domine*, Arise O Lord.

Why 41 Papal Theses against Martin's 95? Many feel Ecken pushed to ensure a swift reply instead of a thoroughly researched one.

To the interested, here is a short summary of the bull:

I Got 41 Counter Theses

and not a one of them are up for debate. If you don't recant I will excommunicate you. please come to Rome with your recantation.

Martin's response to the 1520 papal bull?

* The papal cows were something else altogether.

He burned it... along with some other books.*

Freddie Dubs didn't send him to Rome. Jan (John) Hus
had been summoned under similar circumstances years
earlier. While Martin was promised safe passage by the
Catholic Church, so was Hus and he was executed. So
Freddie Dubs asked the Emperor if Martin could defend
himself on his own soil. Let the Pope send people to
Germany.**

* Should we be worried because our little cucumber is all grown up yet he
hasn't left the brine? A little more vinegar couldn't hurt?
** Martin being German is one of the few things not disputed in his life.
Even if Germany wouldn't be formalized for a very long time.

Martin would appear at Worms (a city in Germany) in April of 1521, but between receiving the papal bull in June 1520 and April he did get some writing in. Here are some of his more influential published works from this time:

To the Christian Nobility of the German Nation (Published August 1520)

Some people in the church were abusing their power for money. Like one bishop having a custom-made cloak that cost thirty times Martin's yearly salary. Too many works of the church had a fee attached, like a spiritual DMV, which heightened the temptation for greed. (Also, please stop literally kissing the Pope's feet.)

On the Babylonian Captivity of the Church
(Published October 1520)

He attacks the Catholic view of the sacraments. Struck from the list are Confirmation (the church recognizes you as a Christian), Ordination (you are now a priest/bishop/nun), Last Rites (blessing before you die) and Marriage as sacraments. Also during this time, only the bread was given to regular people during Communion. The cup was reserved for the clergy. Martin argued that everyone should be given both. For everyone keeping score at home: that leaves Confession, Baptism and Communion as sacraments.

On the Freedom of a Christian
(Published November 1520)

Martin starts off by suggesting that he and the Pope team up to destroy the papacy.* He also answers the question often posed to him: "If works don't save us, why do anything good at all? Why not just go to pleasure island assured we will be saved from donkey form in the end?"

His answer: You are saved so that you can do good works. As Christians it's because Jesus loves you that you do good, not you doing good so Jesus will love you. (Or at least not smite you.)

* That went over just as well as you think it did.

April came and Martin headed out to Worms to respond to the papal bull. He felt, strangely, his appearance at Worms would be the debate he had tried to start three years earlier. Martin* apparently didn't take into account:

- He had already been to three disputations.
- He had been explicitly told he was a Bohemian.
- He was given 41 reasons why he was wrong.
- A theological debate wouldn't usually be hosted by the Emperor at an Imperial Diet (gathering of the highest ranking people in the Empire).
- Jan Hus was given a "similar opportunity" and was executed at that opportunity.

All of this should have clearly been evidence that, "this isn't the debate you're looking for."** Since Martin arrived at Worms with much fanfare, he thought this was

* As well as several Martin biographies.
** What he should have thought was, "I have a bad feeling about this."

his moment and he was going to change the system from the inside.

When he appeared before the Imperial Diet, there was a table piled with his writings on it. The debate Martin was expecting* went like Jan Hus's council except for two things:

He was asked two questions instead of one:

Ecken: "Marty, did you write these?"

Ecken: "Do you recant?"

Remember last time he was asked to recant? Our pickle bravely and resolutely ran away. Has he learned anything new? What did he do this time when he was asked to recant?

---

* No one expected the Imperial Diet. Its chief weapon was surprise. And fear. Their two best weapons were surprise and fear. And ruthless productivity!

He asked to sleep on it.* Surprisingly, they allowed this and the next day, he famously said... well probably said...

Here's the thing, when you hear a quote from a non-English speaker that sounds awesome in English, it's probably not a direct translation. Here is how it has come down to us in English:

* Well, he asked for a day to prepare a defense.

are you crazy? I will follow what I have read in the Scriptures and my conscience. HERE I STAND, i can do no other.

So the Emperor condemned him to death.

difference #2

He was a given one-and-one-half fortnights* to get his affairs in order. Hus was given many opportunities to recant between his trial and martyrdom/death but was never allowed to leave.

Martin headed back to Wittenberg. No idea what, if any, kinds of affairs he was having. However, if death is certain and you have the opportunity, why not take the chance to leave?

That's when he was kidnapped.

Pro tip: If you are going to be kidnapped, be kidnapped by Freddie Dubs. Remember him? He's the political leader of Martin's corner of Germany. Real class act that Freddie Dubs. He does it right. The idea here is that it's better to be kidnapped by your rich and influential friends than to be executed by the state. At least consider it as a rule of thumb. Or a rule to keep your thumbs.**

* Google it.
** At least, when that friend is Freddie Dubs.

With Martin being "held against his will" he *can't* return at the appointed time. The end of May 1521 comes and goes. The Emperor then signs the death sentence, known as the Edict of Worms, and Martin is now condemned. All of his books are to be burned. He is also not allowed to be alive. Achievement unlocked: his teachings are now considered heretical by both the Emperor and the Pope. Few people in history have accomplished this.

bucket list

- ☑ MULTIPLE DEATH SENTENCES
- ☑ BECOME A HERETIC
- ☐ FINISH TATTOO SLEEVE
- ☐ GET THE BAND BACK TOGETHER
- ☐ GET POPS' APPROVAL

Martin has been kidnapped and placed "illegally" under house arrest. So what do you do when you're stuck in Wartburg Castle with no iPhone? You grow a beard, call yourself Junker Jorg (Knight George) and you write.

Well, first you translate.

Well, first you take Erasmus's parallel Greek/Latin New Testament and translate it into German.

Since 1199, translating the Bible into vulgar* languages had been de facto forbidden.** However, when you're a dead man walking and someone was kind enough to invent the movable type printing press, what have you got to lose?

* Vulgar: *adj* language regular people actually use.
** Not that regulating what gets to call itself a Bible is a bad thing.

With so much illiteracy amongst most people and so much reliance on Latin amongst the learned, regular folks had started to develop a lot of strange ideas. Even local clergy weren't always immune from this. For instance, some people believed that Jesus was born via Mary's ear. The usual method of being born would have somehow defiled the Messiah.

What could be more useful than a New Testament you could actually read? Especially, if you thought that you didn't need the clergy to interpret it for you? If only the clergy can read what you're arguing with the Pope about, that puts you at a bit of a disadvantage.

Pope Leo X died in late 1521 and Adriaan Florensz became Pope Adrian IV.* The new Pope went to the Emperor and said he needed to enforce the Imperial Diet at Worms, and promptly.**

Martin returned to Wittenberg after Easter.*** He returned to the Black Order, shaved his beard, resumed the tonsure and began preaching. A tonsure is the haircut you think of when you think of monks. It was meant to represent a crown.

* Last un-Italian Pope until Pope John Paul II in 1978. Also one of the few Popes to retain their baptismal name after becoming Pope.
** His request came with the promise of church reforms.
*** It's unclear when the death sentence of Worms ends. Some put it during the Imperial Diet early in 1522, others have it being lifted later in 1523. Either way, he feels safe enough to travel in Germany and returns to Wittenberg.

Meanwhile, the city had gone bonkers while Martin was gone. People weren't just rebelling against papal authority but also against political authority. Martin traveled around the area preaching in an effort to help. (It only made things worse, more on that later.) While the death sentence was still in effect, Martin was able to travel safely within the domain of Freddie Dubs.

Martin published the New Testament translation in September of 1522. It sold like crazy pants.* Think about all of its features:

- It was an affordable book
- It was in German
- It was the New Testament translated from Greek, not the Vulgate (the accepted Latin translation)
- It was written by a convicted criminal and enemy of the church
- It was wireless
- It required no monthly subscription

When Martin wasn't traveling or writing or sleeping he was probably preaching. It is estimated he preached about 7000 times** over the course of his life.

* Martin's royalties per book sold? Zero guldens, which helped the book be affordable. It also kept Martin from looking like he was only in it for the guldens.
** Almost more impressive, is that we still have around 2300 written copies of them. In the pre-internet, pre-nuclear, pre-electrical, pre-gas, pre-steampunk age, having so many is incredible.

While Martin was doing his thing, so were the Pope and the Emperor. In 1523, the Imperial Diet met in Nuremberg and officially told Martin to stop (again):

OFFICIAL LIST OF THINGS YOU BETTER NOT EVER DO AGAIN EVER OR ELSE

Preaching

Teaching

Talking

Anything not (Roman) Catholic

Sincerely,
The Holy Emperor and his Excellency, the Pope
XOXO

Normally receiving such a demand would be a big deal, but it was a big improvement from being told to be dead.

It will come as no surprise to the uncommon geeks reading this book that a person who has survived a lightning storm, an austere monk's life, a 1600-mile round-trip journey without a car or plane, being excommunicated, living without 4G LTE, being sentenced to death by the Holy Roman Empire and being kidnapped... wasn't going to be stopped by a piece of paper.

By the summer, Martin had a new piece published. The new piece was about how he was conducting church services. A few of the new features included:

Church Services in the Common Tongue!

Congregational Song!

The Bible in German!

Everything goes vulgar! The whole service, including the singing and the sermon all in regular-people German. No advanced degrees required. While we're at it, the singing will be done by the congregation as well as the choir. Why not add the congregation to the choir now that they can sing along in their mother tongue?

In 1524, another Imperial Diet was held. Again, they banned Martin from doing his thing. He didn't seem to notice.

After Martin ignored the latest Diet, he published a songbook so folks could sing (in German) during church.*

We've yet to discuss this until now, but Martin loved music.

Loved, loved, loved it.

Totally should have considered marrying music.

He could sing and play the lute. In his school days he caroled for money. Which gave him the money that paid for him to do something called eating.** Pops Hans only covered tuition.

* Not a chapter book.
** Caroling used to be year-round, they'd sing anything that got them coin.

We'll expand more on his love of music later, now a little break from all of this ~~Marcia, Marcia, Marcia~~ Martin, Martin, Martin.

D.E.R. had been working on a chapter book of his own. In the fall of 1524, he published a book to specifically discuss and counter Martin's big ideas. It was not nailed to any doors as far as we know.

The Freedom of the Will was put forward to say that man have a hand in saving himself.* Martin had been clear that no one could save themselves, it was only by grace from God.**

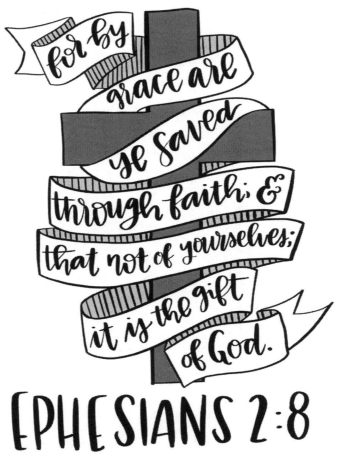

for by grace are ye saved through faith; & that not of yourselves; it is the gift of God.

EPHESIANS 2:8

D.E.R. countered Martin with, "why would God put forward rules if they are inherently impossible to keep?" He felt people were co-conspirators with God: He had the grace and we were to bring the faith.

* Or herself
** *Sola Gratia*

Martin took his time in responding. So much time that people thought that he didn't have a response to D.E.R.*

Why was it taking so long to write a reply to D.E.R.? These two were well matched intellectually and sharp-witted. It certainly sounds like the kind of thing people would have happily bought tickets to.

* Read as: people thought Martin lost and didn't even have a witty retort.

LUTHER VS. D.E.R.

EPIC THROW DOWN

Martin, was distracted. Earlier in 1524, he had helped some nuns escape from their convent. He was publishing that monkeries and nunneries should be closed and people shouldn't be forced into the single life — and he was helping make that happen. This was 16th century Europe, so when you have a bunch of single ladies recently freed from the abbey, they have a cultural expectation that someone will put a ring on it.*

* The more things change... the more things stay the same.

Martin had a lot irons in the fire in his personal life. For example, in June of 1525 he marries one of those escaped nuns. She asked him and one other man to marry her and Martin got there first.* Between marriage and the German Peasants' War of 1524-1525, he was more than distracted.

In December 1525, he finally published his response to D.E.R.

* Not exaggerating.

Martin called it, *On the Bondage of the Will,* and with it he left it all on the field.

The preface of the book actually included a thank-you to D.E.R. because he totally got what Martin was all about. Many people thought the Reformation was about papal authority or the rights of the state or the proper Christian view of kissing.*

* Are you reading between the lines here? Especially you parents who are dutifully reading this book aloud to their children because you're good Christians, or at least hip ones. High-five!

D.E.R. understood Martin was arguing the nature of salvation. He challenged Martin at his core. Frankly,* Martin appreciated the directness.

On the Bondage of the Will is Martin's groundbreaking work. By a mile. Whether people can save themselves solo or are equal partners or are totally dependent on God is a big deal. Martin said we are totes in need of God, otherwise God is not independent of people.

This book is not the most important thing he would do, which is why you haven't read it.** But the work is far from inconsequential.

ULTRA RARE MERIT BADGE!

I Read on the BONDAGE of THE Will

So who won? You decide. If you want to find something to really divide the Christian family, get very specific on how salvation happens and watch a fight break out.

* Germanly? Saxonly? Martin wasn't French after all.
** If you have read it, feel free to go dust off your merit badge collection before proceeding. Go post a picture on social media, we'll wait. #IReadBOTWMeritBadge

Chapter 5 (minus a half)

Intermezzo (Brief But Delightful Musical Interlude)

Let's take a pause from linear storytelling to discuss a different, but related, story that will also be told linearly. While Martin is rightly well known for breaking stuff, there are some other subjects he should also be known for. For this chapter, we are going to discuss music for the most part (and touch on the arts in general).

The Catholic Church during this time period was a big patron of the arts. Big big big. The vast majority of reformers were not. Not not not.

For some it was because "art" was an excuse for extravagant materialism while for others it was that art was too close to idolatry.*

Martin was only mildly concerned with the former and thought little of the latter. He had a very high view of art, especially music. For him music was second only to the Word of God.

* After all, you can't spell idol*arty* without art. (But in German you can pretty much spell götzendienst without kunst.)

We don't know if the Luder family was a musical one. As a student, he had at least some musical training. He even caroled for food money. In Martin's time period, caroling was year-round and the tunes were selected for their ability to make money, not limited to holiday music. He also learned to the play the lute.*

His musical talents were utilized for the daily chants almost from the beginning of joining the monastery.

* It was as close as he could get to an electric guitar back then. Just imagine him with a long tonsure, head banging with some fantasy metal.

While most reformers were at best, *cautious* of music, Martin was a firm believer that music was a good gift that we should enjoy. While he didn't believe it was invulnerable to evil, it was too good to box up out of fear. So while others were making rules to keep music down, Martin enjoyed music for music's sake. He saw no need to confine it to only "Christian" music or to church services.

You could say that Martin didn't really like people who didn't like music because it was something he said, but he never had trouble finding reasons not to like people... so it might not be particularly relevant.

In 1524, he published three different books on music:

Etlich Cristlich lider / Lobgesang und Psalm (*Some Christian songs / canticle and Psalm*) later referred to as *Achtliederbuch* (*Eightsongbook*)*

Next, *Erfurt Enchiridion* (*Erfurt Handbook*) was published and was also immediately competing with itself on the shelves, because two versions were published. One had a bonus song.** Martin wrote most of the music. This was not a hymnal, however, this was music for everywhere. Good music was good all of the time. Martin made no distinction between "secular" and "sacred" music. When couldn't you use a good tune to aid in spiritual contemplation and education?

Eyn geystlich Gesangk Buchleyn (*A Sacred Song Booklet*) came next. It was an upgrade from his previous works both in length and musicality, with 24 hymns by Martin and 8 by others. These were hymns not written in unison, unlike his previous works. This book became the de facto hymnal of the Lutheran movement as it was reprinted half a dozen times with additional hymns added along the way. The final edition compiled by Martin in 1545 was called *Geystliche Lieder* (*Sacred Songs*).

---

* Possibly because it had eight songs in the book? Scholars can't agree, it's a mystery we may never solve.
** Or impostor song?

Songs had other powerful benefits that Martin appreciated. While his German New Testament was rather affordable, songs could be spread for free through singing,* he could spread his ideas to the regular people of Germany and teach them at the same time. Even a largely illiterate people can teach each other songs.

You might have been told that he diabolically/ingeniously used drinking songs as the basis for some of his hymns. People who have done thoughtful, meaningful research have concluded that he did use songs in bar form. Just not the bar you're thinking of. Bar as in the musical unit of measurement. Not drinking songs because they were drinking songs.

Music bAR
another kind of bAR
THE
Research
BAR & GRILL

* It's as close as they could get to social media.

Martin had no issues with popular music* and did use some of their melodies. Those melodies might have been sung at venues where alcohol was consumed. He didn't discriminate if he liked a melody or tune. Martin found music to be inherently emotional and embraced that as one of its virtues, not a Pandora's box.

Music would not be stifled in Germany, not at church or in the home. Martin ended Latin singing in the Protestant church, and instead adopted congregational singing. It's quite possible that since his music didn't require professional singers, this was used as evidence that he was using "tavern melodies" in church.

Martin's style encompassed complex counterpoints to rustic bar tunes. He wrote dozens of hymns and several parts of the new liturgy. His most enduring hymn would come sometime between 1527 and 1529, *A Mighty Fortress Is Our God*.

In reviewing church history, it's easy to find great leaders who feared the arts and great villains who gave us reasons to. Martin stands in the face of that archetype. He felt that the power of music to touch people's emotions was given by God, not the devil. People's ability to connect to music was valuable, not dangerous. He is almost unique within church history for this perspective at this point in time.

* He had his favorite Meistersingers, similar to singer-songwriters today.

118

Sola Rock'n'Roll might not be the sixth sola, but Martin's high view of music should not be overlooked. The Reformation drastically changed how music was treated during church services. This was no accident, Martin made sure it had a thoughtful place during Sunday services.

CHAPTER 5

Prime Time

In 1517, Martin asked some questions.
In 1522, he translated a New Testament for all.*
In 1524, the peasants revolted.

Specifically, the peasants in southwest Germany.**
Sometimes when you give a large group of people who
feel oppressed the idea that they can throw off some

* German-reading people.
** For those of you keeping score, Martin is in northeast Germany.

oppression... well, they might try to throw off *all* the authority and oppression. Go big or be oppressed.

Within a year the revolt spread to most of Germany. As it turned out, the peasants weren't very interested in being oppressed and they were interested in this Renaissance concept of going big.

Now, here's a question... do you think of Martin as:

A nobleman?

A peasant?

Middle class?

Whose side would he choose in this revolt? Today we tend to think that socioeconomic oppression marketed as divine right is silly. Martin was reforming everything he could get his hands on, how about this?

Nope.

He first wrote *Admonition to Peace* (probably late 1524) in which he told the peasants to cut it out, that violence wasn't the answer and they should peacefully submit to the authorities/vile oppressors. Strangely, it didn't help the situation and it quickly became a situation of everyone behaving badly.

Some of the princes counter-revolted. People were killing each other all over the place. About a month after *An Admonition to Stop it You Naughty Peasants** the conflict ended at the Battle of Frankenstein.**

At least 3,000 peasants died versus only a handful of the princes' mercenaries, and Martin responded with *Against the Murderous, Thieving Hordes of Peasants.****

We'll leave out a lot of the potty-mouth stuff. In terms of things Martin didn't rock, this is was one of those moments.

---

* My translations of *An Admonition to Peace*.
** Actually the Battle of Frankenhausen.
*** Actual title, no sarcasm required.

His contemporaries felt the work had a lot of swear words, so Martin published *An Open Letter on the Harsh Book Against the Peasants.* He might have meant it as a defense of his previous work, an explanation, a politician's "I didn't mean what I said." But, Martin stood his ground and said even meaner things.

The whole revolting situation killed a lot of people (mostly peasants) and animals. The peasants did *NOT* rejoice. The worse was yet to come, for him and for the German people.

You may recall that Martin was generally a preaching machine.* He took a big chunk of time off in 1527** because of several major scares*** related to health issues. Between the work, the movement, his family and the big scary thing that happened next... the surprise wasn't his poor health, it was that he survived and got back in the preaching saddle.

After he regained his strength, he found himself well just in time for the plague**** to strike Wittenberg.

* He probably preached in his sleep, just to keep his skills sharp.
** In this case "off" means he called it retirement from his calling to preach.
*** By scares I mean there were several nights he thought would be his last. No reports of any hastily made vows to Saint Anne on these occasions.
**** This is the big scary thing alluded to in the previous paragraph.

How long does a pastor/preacher/leader/troublemaker stay in town when there's a pandemic no one understands? Freddie Dubs told him to get out of town until things cooled off. His pregnant wife, his young firstborn* and everyone else was in danger.

For many it comes as no surprise that when the plague came to town, suddenly how powerful or perfect the Pope was became a secondary issue. Martin did what he did second best. He wrote. In November, a shorter piece entitled *Whether One May Flee From a Deadly Plague* was published. His answer?

Things got real bad and at one point in 1527 he wrote to Philip** that he had spent more than a week in hell.*** These were issues out of his control, for someone so resolute, so independent, there is no greater test. It was sometime between 1527 and 1529 when he wrote

* Firstborn male. Also his firstborn child.
** Philip Melanchthon was his right-hand man.
*** Hell isn't a dirty word for some of you. But is there a bigger curse word? Certainly not for Martin.

his most famous hymn, *A Mighty Fortress Is Our God*. Remember, he was a man who preached early and often, to himself. Given all that led up to *A Mighty Fortress*, it's easy to imagine this too was him preaching to himself, just with a melody.

Martin found the general level of Christian knowledge to be somewhere between really bad and satanic. The clergy, even those decidedly with him, weren't much better. He took a move from the Catholic playbook and wrote *The Small Catechism* in early 1529.

A catechism is a learning tool. In Protestant circles, they are typically written in question-and-answer format. For example:

Catechisms are often used for teaching children as they are easy to memorize and useful to annoy the children.

A couple of months later, he would follow it up with *The Large Catechism*. *The Large Catechism* contained less questions with answers and was mostly detailed answers. Please, no questioning the answers.

It's likely that he was putting these together because while the division from the Catholic Church hadn't been quite legalized...

Martin didn't see that as a reason to not start dividing up his division.

Huldrych (or Ulrich) Zwingli and the Swiss reformers weren't going along with Martin on what happened during Communion. Martin was firm that Christ's body and blood were present alongside the bread and wine.* Ulrich, or Huldrych, let's call him Z... held that Communion is merely ceremonial, you are just eating bread and wine. Since Jesus is at the right hand of God, He can't also be present with the bread and wine** and He isn't going to fly around all over the world every Sunday like Santa Claus so people can have Communion.

* If you ever wanted to get Martin's dander up, call it consubstantiation.
** Why can't He be in two places at once?

Late in 1529* Martin and Z met, named the meeting the Marburg Colloquy, argued, agreed about a lot of things, but *someone* drew a line in the sand about Communion. Which resulted in another name being added to the list of people Martin didn't like.

In 1530 the Emperor called the Diet of Augsburg** hoping to figure out a way the empire could move forward with the German Protestants being German, Protestants, alive and without death sentences. This is the beginning of legal status for the movement.*** Unfortunately, Martin was still a fugitive and had to send Philip Melanchthon in his stead. There was much

* Also in 1529 we first see the word Protestant.
** All of this religious feuding was really hampering his efforts to defend against/invade the Ottoman empire.
*** Official peace between the Lutherans and the Holy Roman Empire wouldn't happen until 1555; the *Augsburg Confession* wouldn't even receive a provisional ruling until 1548. It was very difficult for everyone involved. It probably contributed to the Emperor abdicating the throne about a year later in 1556.

wrangling and discussion and politics and the forming of the Schmalkaldic League and confutation and apologies that were more #sorrynotsorry than anything else. In the end, Martin declared he felt Philip did a better job than he would have. It had something to do with it being better not to send the bull into the china shop.

It was here that the *Augsburg Confessions* was started. In this context, a confession is a summary of beliefs, useful for answering questions and drawing lines in the sand. Written by Melanchthon, the *Augsburg Confession* is one of the foundational documents of the Lutheran denomination.

In 1531, Martin was feeling old before his time. His off-and-on health issues flared up and he took another long leave from preaching. However, he was far from done; Martin continued to do as much work as his health would allow.

Fun side note: Sometime in 1532, he was given his former monastery building as a home. It had 40 rooms on the first floor.* Sooo... he was amply able to receive visitors, students, theater troupes, choirs, entire villages and unicorn trainers.

* YOLO! But seriously I hope that the house came with help. His oldest was only six at this point.

Many biographies on Martin end at the Diet of Worms or the Diet of Augsburg. At the Diet of Worms he took a stand, and at the Diet of Augsburg his movement took a stand. While these moments were pivotal, it's cutting the story short to end at either place. If you want to end at his prime, it should be at what happened next.

In theory, Christianity could have been defeated by the Renaissance. Between the riches of the merchant class and a rising independent, academic elite, the Church easily could have been relegated to the past. Yet, when the humanists touting *ad fontes* (the source languages) came to examine the Latin translations of the Bible, people like Martin were not caught with their proverbial pants down.

How do you not get caught with your pants down? You have to use a belt.

What did Martin do? He thought to himself, *"I'm not afraid of a fight, I'll wear the belt."* He spat in his hands, girded his loins and made the truth available to more people:

He translated the Bible into German.

In late 1534, he published the first edition of the Wittenberg Bible. It was translated into regular-people* German. Scholarship, revision and new editions would be an ongoing project for the rest of his life.**

A Bible that people could read, in every home, was better than a chicken in every pot, as far as Martin was concerned. If you could read (and trust) a translation,*** your pastor/priest/guru/father/reverend/shaman could love, lead and guide but was no longer a gatekeeper between you and God. This later becomes formally known as the priesthood of all believers. In the Old Testament, there was a priestly class prescribed by God but now, according to the reformers, all Christians had complete and direct access to God because of the death and Resurrection of Jesus Christ.

Martin leads Christianity into the Renaissance by giving the Bible to people in their own language. He wasn't the first to translate into a vulgar language, but his work is one of the most influential. A wave of translations followed over the next 50 years, in enough languages that allowed most of Europe to read the Bible in their respective native tongues. This amount of translation wouldn't be seen again until the 20th century.

* Some would say, "vulgar."
** Again, no royalties.
*** And if you can't trust the translation, you'll have to trust your Greek/Hebrew/Aramaic professor.

The Renaissance is known for a lot of things, but what it should be chiefly known for is the first age of marketing. They had the clever idea to name themselves the "Age of Enlightenment" and the age before them the "Dark Ages." Martin and his contemporaries didn't fear the technology or the discoveries of the Renaissance, instead they boldly marched into it. They weren't concerned that their God was going to be caught without a belt.

As far as they were concerned, God invented belts.

CHAPTER 6

The Matchmaker Meets His Match

You've may have been wondering about a certain someone, at least since Chapter Five. It is... uncommon... for a woman to ask two men to marry her.* Let's discuss.

No surprise that we've singularly focused on Martin up to this point. Now it's time for the spotlight to shift to Katharina von Bora, his wife. Her name should stick out more in history, since she is proof of the old adage:

---

* Calm down. It's also uncommon for a man to ask two women.

BEHIND every great ~~MAN~~ person ~~is a~~ ~~woman~~ ARE other PEOPLE.

The Martin you have been learning about owes her a great debt, so he can take a seat for a bit. Their relationship is important. Possibly vulgar-Bible-translating important.

Born into a noble but cash-poor family, Katharina was given to the church* as a tithe and to be a nun, and because it was cheapest dowry available.**

* There were more than 10 children in her family. She wasn't the tenth but who's counting?
** The truth feels snarky enough.

Funny thing about a nunnery in the 16th century,* it was a place where a woman could be educated, and given leadership training and experience without incurring negative social consequences.**

Katharina caught wind of a radical, outspoken monk who left the monastery and in 1522 wrote harsh words against the foundational vows of monastic**** life. People began leaving the monasteries and nunneries. The monks left the monasteries and found jobs. The nuns...

* And there aren't many funny things...
** If words like segregation and celibacy come to mind, you're not wrong, they just also apply to monks.***
*** But not necessarily to priests.
**** And nun-nastic? Hmm, not quite as fantastic.

Oh wait, this is still the 16th century...

The nuns hope their families have additional money available for a (second) dowry so they can get married because their leadership training doesn't do any good on their resume...

They also hope they aren't too old to get married...

How are you ever supposed to find a man in a market suddenly flooded with nuns?

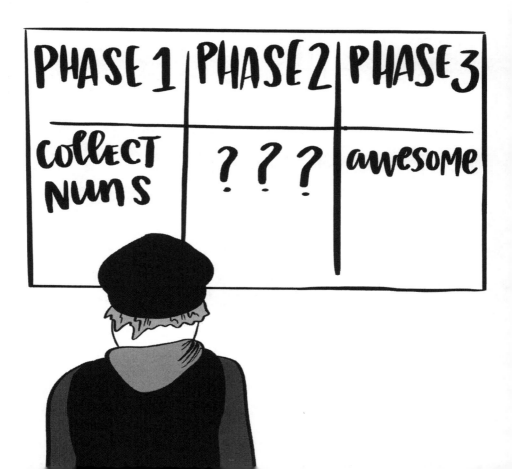

A certain monk apparently didn't think through the macroeconomic implications of "freeing" a group of people that society didn't have a transition strategy for.

While some monasteries shut down (and handed over the land to the nearest German official) with little fuss, the convents weren't always so interested in Protestantism. Some were downright hostile.

Sure Katharina's order was austere, but some were rather luxurious if the nun was personally wealthy. It was the

highest social rank they could attain outside of marriage. What better future was Martin offering?

Katharina's nun-nastic lifestyle was not luxurious or her choice. She probably didn't need a lot of persuading to ditch those vows. At 24 years old, this was the prime time for her to get a husband.* While we have little information about her at this time, her later actions indicate that she was a tough cookie.

So how did she and 11.141529 of her bravest friends escape?

 Was it the butler using the key to unlock the library window?

 Was it the gardener and his ladder helping them scale the wall?

 Was it the fishmonger who smuggled them out in barrels?

* If you thought prime time would have been much younger, you're thinking of the medieval ages, silly. This is the 16th century we're talking about, we have muzzle-loading rifles and everything. You still don't have jet packs.

 Was it outside money bribing the guard at the gate?

 You might have heard the escape involved a waterfall. Currently, there isn't a convenient waterfall between the convent in Nimbschen and Wittenberg, but it would have made the whole thing more cinematic.

Either way, no one wrote it down. Or none of the writings remain. Or the writings are in a time capsule somewhere waiting to be discovered. But at the end of the day, here's what we do and don't know:

- We don't know how it happened
- We don't know who else was involved
- We don't know how a group of women who took a vow of silence even discussed it
- We don't know the exact number of escapees
- We are pretty sure that Katharina von Bora escaped
- We are pretty sure Martin was involved, but not as sure as we are of Katharina's escape

Somewhere around a dozen nuns went AWOL on April 5, 1523. The evening of April 4, the day before Easter, everything seemed normal at the convent. Since it was

Easter Eve, there was more work than usual and the day ended later than normal for everyone. Katharina and her friends celebrated the Resurrection of Jesus by leaving their beds empty.*

The next day they traveled, presumably by wagon, for some 26 nautical miles** before they finally stopped at Wittenberg.

Over the years, Martin changed his tune a little regarding quitting nunneries. Later he would change his advice from "get thee out of the nunnery" to: "make sure you have some viable means outside the convent before you get out of the frying pan and find yourself in the fire." Martin hadn't learned that lesson yet.

* Or strategically the nuns felt that whoever was likely to stop them would have their guard down due to the holiday.
** Did you have to look this one up?

Since Internet dating was still technically forbidden,* Martin and his team went to find husbands for the holy harem. Katharina quickly found a suitor and a suitably noble one at that. Mr. Hieronymus (Ronnie) Baumgartner of Nuremberg and Katharina pretty quickly became an item.

Ronnie went home to Nuremberg and everyone seemed to think he would be returning with a marriage proposal once he got his parents' blessing. Until the months started to pass. Martin wrote a letter to see if he could help.

Dear Ronnie,
    Put up or shut up.
She's still in love with you.
   – awaiting your
       prompt reply,

          Martin Luther
PS: seriously man,
    what's your deal?

* Due to the fact that it technically didn't exist.

Everyone got their answer in the spring of 1525, when the engagement of Ronnie and Sibylle Dichtel von Tutzing was announced. She, like, had a dowry and everything... Sorry, Katharina.

Boy she was bummed, and while last year she was 24, now she was 25. She was quickly going from the perfect age for marriage to old maid, even in the early modern period.*

Martin had a possible suitor, a pastor at a nearby town named Kaspar Glatz (KG). KG had one very strong qualification and one very strong disqualification. (He had a reputation for being a jerk.)

qualifications	**disqualifications**
SINGLE MAN HAS JOB	I DON'T LIKE HIM

So Katharina asked Martin's friend for help in coming up with a new plan. Nikolaus von Amsdorf, Nik V, asked how KG, a learned man of the faith was somehow not good enough for her. *If you want a peek into who Katharina is, here's a good moment to remember:*

* Nevertheless, she persisted.

Her response was to propose that either Nik V or Martin could marry her. But KG could take a hike.

This (16th century) woman who had spent a significant amount of time as a nun, with no money and a family that wasn't interested, had just asked two men to marry her.

Martin was clearly pro marriage but hadn't gotten around to looking for a lady for himself. This might have had something to do with the wanted posters that were on display outside of his cozy corner of Germany.

Who wants to marry an excommunicated man who could be captured and killed by either the Pope or the Emperor at any time? Like most single men, Martin had some wonderfully romantic yet untested views about marriage and women.*

You might think it would all be worth it to marry someone famous/important, but at this point it was only 1525. While the 133 theses, some hymnals, and a German New Testament are published, it was decades away from the legalization of Protestantism. He was a wanted man.** They haven't even named what was happening *Protestantism* yet. He's also wasn't great at the whole money thing. No gambling debts or anything like that, but you know these big-picture types... no love of spreadsheets or changing the bed straw.

* Of course, no single woman has *ever* had wonderfully romantic yet untested views about marriage and men.
** And not the "dead or alive" kind. Just dead.

There is a lot of speculation about why Martin married her. Was he always going to marry the first nun who didn't find a suitor? Did he pity her? Did he see it as duty? Did God predestine them? Was the only way to get Martin down the aisle to force his hand?

WHO CARES
WHAT MARTIN THINKS?

Let's talk about Queen ~~Bey~~ K and her perspective. She had serious cajones* and she knew that life with Martin would be an adventure. Her life had been scripted so far and he was a guarantee of throwing the script out of the window. What if some sneaky script showed up? Martin would probably burn it.

Biographers tend to focus on how unromantic or romantic it all might have been. They miss the real story by trying to make their relationship fit into a movie-style romance or makeover fantasy. People want them to be googly eyed at each other or need a scene in which, after they are married, she takes off her glasses, tosses her hair back and he "gets it." Maybe they are looking for a moment

* Is that the Spanish word for ovaries? It's Latin for spheres of courage. Lo siento, pero no hablo espanol. Latine mea malum.

when he gives her his library, revealing Martin isn't quite the beast he appears to be.

If you can imagine that Queen K wasn't a shrinking violet, then it's not a stretch to imagine her attracted to Martin's wildness. Doesn't even have to be romantic (but it, like, totally could be).

Look.

Here's a man who is changing the world, has a death sentence and fearlessly writes whatever he pleases.

Here's a woman who wasn't groomed to be a wife. She was groomed to be a functioning member of a team. Who was brave enough to covertly conduct an escape mission with no endgame planned. A woman who would rather be alone in the 16th century than be with a man she didn't like.

Seeing the two of them together just isn't that hard. Quit quibbling about her being a nontraditional wife, Martin was as traditional as a pig at passover. In Queen K, Martin had met his match.

While we're reforming things, Martin (unintentionally?) reforms weddings and then marriages.

*Skip ahead to page 156 to avoid all of the kissing. It's a mostly tasteful discussion. But you have been warned.

You might recall that in 1520 Martin wrote *On The Babylonian Captivity of the Church* and declared that marriage wasn't a sacrament. Even before that in 1519, he published *Sermon on the Estate of Marriage*. Everyone agreed marriage was a big deal. Here's the thing about this point in history: while a considered sacrament, getting into a marriage was essentially deregulated and getting out of a marriage was heavily regulated. This view applied to the people, the church and the state.

At the time, teenagers could choose to get married. It was pretty straightforward to make the sacrament of marriage official.

Yep.

Kissing.*

Step 1) One asked the other.
Step 2) They said yes.
Step 3) Then they consummated the relationship.

In the eyes of the church (and the state) they were now married. License, ceremony, parental input, etc. were not required.

* See? Tasteful. You're welcome.

This lack of formal process clogged up the courts. Here are just a few ways this would go wrong...

- Occasionally, step four was, "parental intervention"
- Sometimes she claimed they were married, but he claimed he was still celibate*
- In some cases, the parents from both sides wanted to disown them both for their decision.

The part where the Church got involved was getting *out* of marriage. It could be difficult and expensive to get a marriage annulled in the eyes of the Church.**

Let's recap:
Formal license: optional
Wedding ceremony: optional
Adulthood: optional

That's just 16th century Christendom in general. In Germany, a wedding ceremony was optional but it tended to happen and be a big to-do.

To be a guest at some of these weddings might have required an interview with the city government — with one of the peculiar questions being whether you had spent an appropriate amount of money on the gift. The government wanted to ensure you didn't spend too much.

* Remember, in 16th century Europe, nothing was better than celibacy, especially if you were a woman.
** Even for the King of England.

Martin was getting married, so he hadn't reformed it yet. Part of the marriage du jour meant having a witness in a formal marriage. A witness to the *kissing*.

Yep.

By having a formal wedding ceremony, and at a church no less, he unintentionally created the template for all the Protestant wedding ceremonies for the entire world. While having the ceremony at a church wasn't required, the pastor was. This all became part of the written liturgy

of how a Protestant marriage started.

Yes, his marriage did involve a witness. *Strangely,* that part didn't become part of the protestant marriage ceremony. Sometimes you have to experience something before you can reform it.

After a little, shall we say, "experience," he decided to reform his views on "kissing." The medieval world saw celibacy as the best state* and even "kissing" within marriage as something to severely limit. He threw that out, said it wasn't sinful and it was okay if married people enjoyed it.

end interlude

Essentially all of the history we have on their marriage are Martin's letters to Queen K. In the letters he refers to her with honorifics such as: Doctor, Preacher, Lord** and Empress and endearments such as sweetheart and beloved. From these letters it's clear that he cared for her deeply.

Martin wasn't full of kindness generally, but he had great respect for her. Once he didn't travel on account of Queen K having a dream the night before that he had died.

* For both men and women, though definitely more for women.
** Not LORD, just Lord.

Martin gave complete control of the finances to her. He asked her to help find a new pastor for a parish by doing the interviews on his behalf while he was traveling.

It would be easy to take the work she did of minding the business of their life and either venerate it or degrade it as woman's work. Either simplification would miss the point. They were a team. Martin the bachelor would not have lived long enough to translate the Bible without her care. She was the doctor he trusted.

Martin and Queen K had mutual respect for each other's strengths and abilities. They were equally matched, regardless of how much romance you do or don't read into it.

CHAPTER 6.5

It's All Downhill From Here

We left Martin holding his translation of the Bible. This first edition was published when he was 52. Unlike his other works, Martin never felt this one was ever truly complete. With the help of a group of translators, this work would take him to the end of his days. The last printed page he would see was a proof for a revised edition of the German Bible more than 10 years later.

In 1535, he became a dean at the Wittenberg University.

Johannes* Bugenhagen took over as pastor of the town church. Martin would act as a backup to Pomeranus, his nickname for Johannes, on occasion. The rest of his teaching and preaching was at the university. While at church he was able to shepherd his town. At the university, he could train the next generation of (Lutheran) pastors.

Amongst preaching, teaching and writing he was also hard at work codifying his church reforms and theology.

* You can't throw a stick in this book without hitting almost a dozen guys named Johann.

160

He was concerned about how low practical theological knowledge was in general. It would take decades for his Small and Large Catechisms to permeate Germany, let alone influence the rest of Europe. So Martin focused on theology and music for the people.

Martin wanted to make sure the Bible was preached and the music was good. The rest he left up to the next generation. He was concerned with the theology of the average German, not the color of the carpets or church governance.

Melanchthon and Pomeranus had the work of putting muscle and skin on top of the nervous system and bone structure Martin had created. They did the work of figuring out the systems of the church. Things like church governance, when services would be, accent walls, etc.

In this time period, we get most of Martin's especially... memorable and *polemic** works. Some of his greatest hits in this category include:

- *On the Councils and the Church* (1539)
- *Appeal for Prayer Against the Turks* (1541)
- *Against Hanswurst* (1541)
- *On the Jews and Their Lies* (1543)
- *Against the Papacy at Rome, Founded by the Devil* (1545)

* Polemic means angry or hostile. In this case it also means full of foul language and sometimes racism.

Modern readers will largely find these works very difficult to understand.* The truth is, plenty of his contemporaries also found it difficult.** It is common today to condemn him for being a potty mouth or try to excuse him (while looking down on him) because foul-mouthed writing was not uncommon in that time.

However, even back then, those close to him were

* After all, most modern readers can't read German or Latin.
** And they far more often could read Latin and German.

concerned. Martin now considered himself to be a man of war, a pioneer, not a man of the cloth. He felt he was going first on the trail and had to battle devils and the people who would divide him from the truth. Martin found himself angry and fueled by that anger. He made no excuses, because Martin felt his pen was an ax and he looked to have others feel the might of his words. Martin's enemy was the devil, why should he be concerned with Satan's feelings? Or the feelings of his minions?*

D.E.R. is quoted to have said of the whole affair:

because of the magnitude of the disorders, god gave this age a violent physician

—D.E.R.

---

* Certainly a very different view than in our own day.

Feel free to decide for yourself.* Was he just a pickle who brined entirely too long? Did he get to heaven and have his mouth washed out with soap? Was he exactly what the Great Doctor ordered? Would anyone else have stood up to the problems of the age?

While his health was rarely not declining, if he was able to stand, he'd preach. If he was able to hold a pen, he'd write. When he finally confessed faith for the last time (remember that Confession is still a sacrament.) He had been laid up in bed for a couple of days. Away from his Queen, in the place of his birth, he died.**

They buried him in front of the pulpit at Wittenberg Castle Church. Where the 95 Theses had (probably) been nailed almost 30 years earlier.

* For further reading on "I heard that Martin Luther said ___" see the next chapter.
** She was concerned for his health. He said she worried too much. He died.

CHAPTER 7

The Man, Some Myths and Legends

You may have heard some awesome and/or awful stuff about Martin. Not to speak ill of the dead, but let's discuss some of the juicy ones here. How much of what you've heard is merely rumor and clickbait as opposed to history? Let's dive in:

Does Martin have any miracles attributed to him?

He does have one miracle, according to R.W. Scribner. He cites a 1717 work entitled *Luther non combustus...**

* You can figure this one out.

which discusses some pictures of Martin that would not burn (even if his books did) in 1521. Scribner cites other incidents of noncombustion in 1634 and 1689. During Martin's life people attempted to discredit this idea by burning him in effigy. The effigies did burn as expected. There are no records that the Catholic Church investigated the veracity of these miracles.

How good was his translation of the Bible?

Can any translation completely escape scrutiny? The most discussed critique at the time was Romans 3:28. Martin added the word "alone" so instead of (in English:) "man is justified by faith apart from the

deeds of the law." He wrote, in German, "man is justified by faith *alone* apart from the deeds of the law."

Martin himself didn't argue this point. He claimed that is how a German person would say the phrase, not because the word "alone" is in the text but because that's the vernacular.

In our time, translations are sometimes grouped as *thought for thought, phrase for phrase* and *word for word*. Martin's was clearly not word for word as some folks today would consider in vogue.

Did he intentionally add "alone" to the Bible? Yep.

Did Martin really nail the 95 Theses to the door of the church?

As discussed earlier, we don't know for sure. The first mention of this was recorded after his death, by Melanchthon, who wasn't there. Martin definitely sent copies of them to Bishop Albrecht, because as a monk, Martin was in the "system" and didn't need to use a public forum to discuss his ideas for reform.

Finally, none of the disputations were held at Wittenberg. If the theses had been nailed there, that's where the disputation would have probably been.

While there is evidence for doubt, there is also evidence

for belief: the theses were not written for an internal audience. Martin addressed them openly to scholars for dispute. If he was writing just to Albrecht or the Pope, then you might have seen an introduction closer to: "Dear Pope, I'm very annoyed at you and have various Internet troll comments to share with you."

While our source wasn't present for the event, Melanchthon was Martin's main man. Remember, when Martin couldn't go to Augsburg to begin legalizing the reformation he sent Melanchthon.

It was a common practice of the time, making the claim unsensational, so it's possible but not certain.

In our modern time, since we don't use church doors in this manner, the whole incident is very foreign. At the time it would have been typical. He was already a published author at the time. No one in our day and age is surprised when a blogger appears on a podcast for an interview. However, in 500 years, people might see this form of broadcast and communication as outdated. Maybe they'll think, "It's so strange what barbarians did back then in the late modern period! Now we can just Thoughtcast™ our ideas into Crowdmind™ and take off on our jet packs!"

When Martin was translating the Bible into German, did he meet the devil?

Almost positively no. At least not by the accounts we have to go on.

Version 1 goes something like this:
Martin is working in the study, when all of a sudden...

The devil appears! Martin looks up, perturbed.

The devil says, "I've come to be mean to you and scare you away from teaching people the true gospel that I've spent so long hiding under a rug. I'm Satan! Mwa-ha-ha." Then he laughs devilishly. So, Martin throws an inkwell at him.

Like ya do.

Martin surely said some intentionally very rude things to the devil. He picks up another inkwell.

The devil cringes, "you almost hit me with that thing! You're not very nice. I'm going to run away before you throw another small nonthreatening object at me!"

With that, Martin Luther successfully scared away the devil.

Version 2 is just as silly.

Martin is working in the study, when all of a sudden...
The devil appears! Martin looks up perturbed.

The devil says, "I've come to be mean to you and scare you away from teaching people the true gospel that I've spent so long hiding under a rug. I'm Satan! Mwa-ha-ha." Then he laughs devilishly and throws an inkwell at Martin.

When Martin doesn't run in terror, the devil is confused. "I don't understand, I've successfully stopped thousands of people from translating the Bible by throwing inkwells. What will I do? Oh no!" (Hopefully, everyone believes that neither Martin nor Satan are afraid of inkwells. If you don't, repent and/or do penance.)

Was Martin the first person to bring a Christmas tree inside and decorate it?

Lots of people and groups, even entire countries lay claim to the origin of the Christmas tree:

- St. George's Church in Selestat, France since 1521
- Estonia and Latvia since 1441

No one disputes that the German people love Christmas. Perhaps it's useful to note that *O Tannenbaum* was not initially German for *O Christmas Tree*, but *O Fir Tree*. Otherwise it would have been *O Weihnachtsbaum*.

Was Martin supportive of Prince Philip having two wives or bigamy in general?

Martin didn't support bigamy in general, but he did agree with the Pope and D.E.R. that in some cases bigamy was less disagreeable than divorce.

Did Martin really say _____ ?

The list of things he might have said is really long. Many of the best and worst all come from the same source.

In 1566 (about 20 years after Martin died) a book titled *Table Talk* was published. This was a compilation by multiple authors' notes of the things Martin "said" around the "dinner" table.* That's right, 20 years after he died some of his students got together and published what essentially would have been all of the social media posts that tagged Martin. It's not in chronological order. Even better, it's written in social media format. Instead of entire stories, it's just quotes, all without context.

* Martin's home had a lot of rooms, but not a formal dining room, but you get the idea.

It wasn't authored by his enemies, but it also wasn't authored by someone close to him like, Melanchthon or Queen K. Many of the more fun Martin quotes, stories, etc. come from this book written by his students. Here's an example of the wild claims made in the book. In *Table Talk*, they claim Martin said that Jesus was a repeat adulterer.

It's a very frustrating book because you can use it to build him up or tear him down, and it's all hearsay. If you want to credit or discredit Martin's beliefs or character, he wrote plenty of that on his own. No hearsay required.

CHAPTER 8

Epilog (That's German for Epilogue)

We have so much source material from Martin's life; our time together has truly only been the briefest of introductions to Martin Luther. There are many great works on his life by thoughtful scholars. Hopefully this has given you an appetite to learn more.

At this point, both Martin's super fans and his haters can see why we picked him for our first Holy Misfit. He is better and worse than you've heard. The world is a different place, not entirely as Martin or his enemies would have it, but different because of the person he was and the choices he made.

Some books for further reading:

- *The Legacy of Luther* — Edited by R.C. Sproul and Stephen J. Nichols
- *Katharina and Martin Luther* — by Michelle DeRusha
- *Here I Stand: A Life of Martin Luther* — by Roland Bainton

Thanks again for coming along for the ride.

About the writing team —

Author Josh Hamon has been known to wear a leopard print coat and slay at karaoke. He wrote this book primarily on his (large, state-subsidized, commuter ferry) boat (to Seattle). He enjoys moonlighting at The Doughnut Dame. (IG: @joshhamon)

Illustrator Brynn James is fueled by tacos, coffee and road trips. She is a folk art painter and textile designer, and she runs a clothing line (brynnjames.com) when she's not doodling or raising her wild children. (IG: @brynnjames)